Vegan Salads

37 Plant Based
Vegan Recipes

Dexter Poin

Come hang out with me on **Instagram @dextersworld.** Here I share all sides to my life, including what I am eating on a daily basis.

If you are interested in more vegan recipes, then check out my pages on Amazon. I can't put clickable links in paperback books obviously. Not yet anyways. But while I am working on that, you can easily find links to many things inside of the eBook versions of all of my books. You can also find links here on my website. Type this into your browser – paradigmpublishingconsulting.com

I write many other things, including fiction. Check out my site.

Garbanzo Beans & Citrus 8

Carrot-Raisin-Pineapple Salad 9

Red Pepper and Broccoli Salad 10

Asian Salad 11

Cucumber Salad 12

Brown Rice Corn Salad 13

Purple Cabbage - Red Onion Salad 14

Oriental Salad 15

Corn Salad 16

Tofu Salad 17

Cucumber - Caper Salad 18

Eggplant Salad 19

Vegan Yogurt - Cucumber Salad 20

Green Pepper - Cucumber Salad 21

Cumin and Lime Bean Salad 22

Chickpea and Eggplant Salad 23

Corn and Pepper Salsa Salad 24

Tomato Lime - Sunflower Seed Salad 25

Grapefruit and Avocado Salad 26

Grated Beet Salad 27

Green Bean and Tomato Salad 28

Zucchini - Scallion Salad 29

Sweet Potato Salad 31

Pineapple Salad 32

Carrot Apple Salad 33

Butter Lettuce Fruit Salad 34

Kumquat-Cucumber Salad 35

Plum Fruit Salad 36

Fruit - Rice Salad 37

Honeyberry Salad 38

Cucumber Island Salad 39

Cantaloupe Salad 40

Jicama Slaw 41

Melon Salad 42

Melon Mint Salad 43

Pear Fruit Salad 44

Grape Cardamom Salad 45

Don't forget to leave me a review for this book! They are always appreciated, and I try & read them all. Thanks in advance.

Garbanzo Beans & Citrus

Ingredients:
- ½ tbsp. olive oil
- Pinch of ground coriander
- 1/3 cup garbanzo beans, rinsed and drained
- 3 Kalamata olives, halved and pitted
- 1 tbsp. lemon juice, 1 tsp. zest
- 2 tbsp. orange juice, 2 tsp. zest
- ½ cup water
- Salt and pepper, to taste
- ¼ cup instant couscous

Directions
1. Heat olive oil in large skillet over medium heat.
2. Add coriander, garbanzo beans, olives, and lemon juice to pan and stir. Continue to cook over medium heat, stirring occasionally.
3. In a separate, small saucepan, add water, orange juice, orange zest, lemon zest, and salt. Bring to a boil and stir in couscous. Cover, remove from heat, and let stand for at least 5 minutes.
4. To serve, fluff couscous with a fork and place in serving dish. Top with garbanzo beans.

Nutritional Information
- Calories: 290
- Total Fat: 10 g
- Saturated Fat: 1 g
- Carbohydrates: 41 g
- Protein: 6.5 g

Carrot-Raisin-Pineapple Salad

Ingredients:
- ¼ cup raisins
- ½ tbsp. apple cider vinegar
- ½ cup shredded carrots
- ½ cup shredded purple cabbage
- ¼ cup pineapple chunks
- 1 tbsp. unsweetened pineapple juice
- Dash ground cinnamon
- Dash ground nutmeg
- Dash Sea salt

Directions

1. Combine raisins and vinegar in a medium bold and let stand 15 minutes.
2. Add carrot and pineapple chunks, stirring well.
3. In a separate bowl, combine pineapple juice, cinnamon, and nutmeg. Pour over carrot-raisin mixture and toss well.
4. Serve immediately, or cover and chill to serve later.

Nutritional Information
- Calories: 108.2
- Total Fat: 0.2 g
- Saturated Fat: 0 g
- Carbohydrates: 25.4 g
- Protein: 1.2 g

Red Pepper and Broccoli Salad

Ingredients:
For salad:
- 1 sweet red bell pepper, chopped
- ½ cup shredded carrots
- 2 large broccoli florets, chopped
- ½ celery stick, finely chopped
- Handful of preferred lettuce

For French Dressing:
- 2 tbsp. lemon juice
- 2 tsp white wine vinegar
- ¼ tsp sea salt
- ¼ tsp. sugar (optional)
- 1/8 tsp. mustard
- Dash of pepper

Directions:
1. To make dressing, put all ingredients in a container with a lid and shake well until incorporated.
2. Put bell pepper, carrots, broccoli, and celery in a large bowl and mix well.
3. Add homemade French dressing and mix again.
4. Cover and chill for 30 minutes.
5. Serve on top of shredded lettuce.

Nutritional Information
- Calories: 115.8
- Total Fat: 0.2 g
- Saturated Fat: 0 g
- Carbohydrates: 28 g
- Protein: 0.5 g

Asian Salad

Ingredients:

- ½ head bok choy, sliced thin
- ¾ cup shredded carrots
- 2 green onions, sliced
- ¾ cup bean sprouts
- ¼ cup chopped cilantro leaves
- ¼ cup seasoned rice vinegar
- ½ tsp. Chinese chili-garlic sauce

Directions:

1. Combine vegetables together in a large bowl.
2. In a separate bowl, mix the rice vinegar and chili-garlic paste until well combined.
3. Pour dressing over vegetables, toss, and serve.

Nutritional Information

- Calories: 143.5
- Total Fat: 1.5 g
- Saturated Fat: 0 g
- Carbohydrates: 28 g
- Protein: 4.5 g

Cucumber Salad

Ingredients:
- 1 large cucumber
- 1 large roma tomato
- 2 green onions
- 1 tbsp. white vinegar
- 1 tbsp. lemon juice
- Salt and pepper, to taste.

Directions:
1. Peel and coarsely chop cucumbers. Chop tomatoes the same size as cucumbers.
2. Thinly slice the green onions but save the green bits for garnish and use the white parts for the actual salad.
3. Toss the cucumber, tomato, and white part of the green onion together and pour white vinegar and lemon juice over the whole mixture.
4. Cover and chill for 30 minutes to allow the vegetables to marinate.
5. Add salt and pepper to taste and serve.

Nutritional Information
- Calories: 132
- Total Fat: 0 g
- Saturated Fat: 0 g
- Carbohydrates: 30 g
- Protein: 3 g

Brown Rice Corn Salad

Ingredients:
For salad:
- ½ cup cooked brown rice
- ½ cup frozen corn kernels (thawed)
- ½ tomato, coarsely chopped
- ¼ cup chopped green bell pepper
- ¼ cup chopped green onions
- 1 tbsp. chopped, fresh dill weed

For dressing:
- ½ tsp. Dijon mustard
- ½ tbsp. water
- ½ tbsp. wine vinegar
- ½ tbsp. soy sauce
- Few dashes of tabasco sauce

Directions:
1. Mix brown rice, corn, tomato, green pepper, green onions and dill weed in large bowl. Set aside.
2. Place the mustard in a small jar. Add a half the water and mix until smooth. Add remaining water, vinegar, soy sauce and tabasco. Mix well.
3. Pour dressing over salad, toss, cover and chill for at least 2 hours before serving for best flavor.

Nutritional Information
- Calories: 185.9
- Total Fat: 1.1 g
- Saturated Fat: 0 g
- Carbohydrates: 38 g
- Protein: 6 g

Purple Cabbage – Red Onion Salad

Ingredients:

½ purple cabbage, shredded
- ½ tomato, diced
- ½ red onion, sliced into rings
- ½ green or red bell pepper, diced
- 2 tbsp. cilantro, chopped
- Pinch of salt and pepper
- ½ lime

Directions:

1. Combine cabbage, tomato, red onion and green bell pepper in a large bowl.
2. Top with cilantro and salt and pepper, to taste.
3. Squeeze lime juice over salad, toss, and enjoy.

Nutritional Information

- Calories: 165.8
- Total Fat: 0.2 g
- Saturated Fat: 0 g
- Carbohydrates: 35 g
- Protein: 6 g

Oriental Salad

Ingredients:
For salad:
- ¼ cup leaf Romaine lettuce, torn
- ¼ cup Chinese cabbage, torn
- ¼ cup bean sprouts
- Handful of trimmed snow peas
- ¼ cup canned bamboo shoots
- 1/8 cup shredded carrots
- ¼ cup chopped broccoli
- ¼ cup thinly sliced celery

For dressing:
- ½ tbsp. soy sauce
- ½ tbsp. rice vinegar
- 1 ½ tsp. water
- Pinch of minced garlic
- Pinch of minced ginger root

Directions:
1. Combine all vegetables in large bowl, toss well, and set aside.
2. Combine the dressing ingredients in a small blender or jar. Shake or blend well until incorporated.
3. Pour dressing over salad, toss to coat.
4. Serve immediately and enjoy.

Nutritional Information
- Calories: 89.5
- Total Fat: 0.3 g
- Saturated Fat: 0 g
- Carbohydrates: 18.5 g
- Protein: 3.2 g

Corn Salad

Ingredients:
For salad:
- ½ cup corn (fresh or canned)
- ¼ cup diced red bell pepper
- 1 scallion, chopped
- ½ cucumber, chopped
- Handful of spinach leaves

For dressing:
- ½ tbsp. apple cider vinegar
- ½ tbsp. mustard
- Pinch of each: turmeric, cumin, and coriander
- Pinch of cayenne
- Salt and pepper, to taste

Directions:
1. Combine vegetables together in large bowl.
2. Combine dressing ingredients in separate container until well-mixed.
3. Add dressing to salad, toss well, and allow to marinate for 10 minutes.
4. Serve and enjoy.

Nutritional Information
- Calories: 125
- Total Fat: 1 g
- Saturated Fat: 0 g
- Carbohydrates: 27 g
- Protein: 2 g

Tofu Salad

Ingredients:
- ½ block firm tofu
- 1 tbsp. low fat vegan mayonnaise
- 1/3 cup nutritional yeast
- 1 stalk celery, chopped
- ¼ cup red bell pepper, chopped
- ½ tbsp. dill weed, chopped
- Pinch of turmeric powder
- Salt and pepper, to taste.

Directions:
1. Press tofu with paper towel to remove excess liquid, place in large bowl, and mash with a fork.
2. Combine tofu chunks with all remaining ingredients.
3. Chill for one hour to allow the flavors to blend.
4. Serve alone or on a bed of lettuce.

Nutritional Information
- Calories: 236
- Total Fat: 4 g
- Saturated Fat: 0 g
- Carbohydrates: 30 g
- Protein: 20 g

Cucumber - Caper Salad

Ingredients:
For salad:
- 3 tomatoes, chopped
- ½ cucumber, diced
- ¼ green bell pepper, thinly sliced
- ¼ onion, chopped
- ½ tbsp. capers

For dressing:
- ¼ cup red wine vinegar
- 1 tbsp. chopped parsley
- 1 tbsp. chopped shallot
- 1 garlic clove, pressed
- Pinch cumin
- Salt and pepper, to taste

Directions:
1. Layer tomatoes, then cucumbers, then bell pepper, then onion, and lastly capers in a glass bowl.
2. In a separate container mix vinegar, cumin, parsley, shallots, and garlic.
3. Pour dressing over vegetables, cover and refrigerate for at least two hours.
4. Toss before serving.

Nutritional Information
- Calories: 158.3
- Total Fat: 0.7 g
- Saturated Fat: 0 g
- Carbohydrates: 35 g
- Protein: 3 g

Eggplant Salad

Ingredients:
- ½ medium eggplant
- ½ medium red bell pepper
- 2 cloves garlic
- Splash of lemon juice
- Salt and pepper, to taste
- Handful of preferred greens (baby spinach)

Directions:
1. To roast the eggplant, first preheat oven to 450 degrees.
2. Puncture the eggplant with a fork in several places and place in oven on a non-stick pan for 45 minutes. Turn every 15 minutes. When done, set aside and allow to cool.
3. Once cooled, scoop out the seeds and drain any juices.
4. To roast the peppers, first turn your oven broiler on.
5. Cut bell pepper in half and stick underneath the broiler until the skin is black.
6. Afterwards, place in bag for 10 minutes to steam. Remove the peel under cold water.
7. Dice the roasted the pepper and the garlic.
8. Mash the eggplant in a bowl and add the red pepper and garlic. Add lemon juice to reduce bitterness.
9. Add salt and pepper.
10. Serve over handful of greens or use as a spread for crackers.

Nutritional Information
- Calories: 102.4
- Total Fat: 0.8 g
- Saturated Fat: 0 g
- Carbohydrates: 21 g
- Protein: 2.8 g

Vegan Yogurt - Cucumber Salad

Ingredients:

- 1 Cup of Vegan Yogurt – Low Fat
- 2 Tbsp. of Vinegar
- 2 tsp. of Sweetener
- ½ tsp. of Dill
- 1 Large Cucumber – Peeled, Sliced Thin
- 4 Tomatoes – Cubed
- 1 Green Pepper – Diced
- ½ Red Onion – Sliced Thin

Directions:

1. Stir in the yogurt, sweetener, vinegar, and the dill.
2. Add the pepper and the salt.
3. Add the tomatoes, cucumbers, peppers, and the onion. Toss it to coat.
4. Cover it and allow it to chill for 2-4 hours. Stir it often. Stir it before you serve it.

Nutritional Information:

- Calories: 200
- Total Fat: 0g
- Saturated Fat: 0g
- Carbohydrates: 40g
- Protein: 10g

Green Pepper - Cucumber Salad

Ingredients:
- 2 Cucumbers
- 4 Tomatoes
- 1 Green Pepper
- 1 Tbsp. of Virgin Olive Oil
- 3 Tbsp. of Lemon Juice

Directions:
1. Dice all of the vegetables.
2. Combine all of the ingredients.
3. Allow it to stand for 30 minutes.

Nutritional Information:
- Calories: 200
- Total Fat: 2g
- Saturated Fat: 0g
- Carbohydrates: 40g
- Protein: 7g

Cumin and Lime Bean Salad

Ingredients:

- 1 Can of Corn
- 1 Cup of Black Beans
- 1 Cup of Chickpeas
- Juice from 3 Limes
- 2 Tbsp. of Virgin Olive Oil
- 4 Tbsp. of Cumin

Directions:

1. Strain all of the canned goods, and then rinse them.
2. Put it in a large serving bowl.
3. Add in the oil and cumin.
4. Mix it well.

Nutritional Information:

- Calories: 208
- Total Fat: 7g
- Saturated Fat: 1g
- Carbohydrates: 28g
- Protein: 6g

Chickpea and Eggplant Salad

Ingredients:

- 2 Eggplants – Cut lengthwise, 1 Inch Slices
- ½ tsp. of Sea Salt – Divided
- 2 Tbsp. of Olive Oil
- ½ tsp. of Pepper
- 16 Ounces of Chickpeas, Drained, Rinsed
- 1 Cup of Cherry Tomatoes – Sliced
- 1 Tbsp. of Parsley – Chopped
- 2 Tbsp. of Red Wine Vinegar
- 2 Tbsp. of Lemon Juice
- 2 Cloves of Garlic – Minced
- ½ tsp. of Lemon Zest

Directions:

1. Layer a baking sheet with paper towels.
2. Place the eggplant on the top in a single layer.
3. Sprinkle it with the salt.
4. Cover it with paper towels.
5. Let the eggplant stand for at least 30 minutes.
6. Rinse each of the pieces and blot it dry.
7. Brush the sides with olive oil.
8. Season it with pepper.
9. Heat the grill to medium heat.
10. Grill the eggplant for 16-20 minutes; only turning once.
11. When the eggplant is cooled off, cut it into ½ inch cubes.
12. Toss the eggplant, the chickpeas, and the parsley in a large mixing bowl.
13. Whisk the oil, vinegar, lemon juice, garlic, and lemon zest together. Pour it over the salad and gently toss it.
14. Allow it to stand for 20 minutes.

Nutritional Information:

- Calories: 345
- Total Fat: 8g
- Carbohydrates: 60g
- Protein: 6g

Corn and Pepper Salsa Salad

Ingredients:

- 1 Ear of Corn –Steamed, Cut from Cob
- 1 Large Tomato – Chopped
- 1 Red Pepper – Chopped
- ¼ Cayenne Pepper
- 1 Tbsp. of Olive Oil
- 2 Tbsp. of Lime Juice
- Dash of Sea Salt
- Dash of Pepper

Directions:

1. Prepare all of your ingredients together in same bowl, and mix.
2. Allow it to stand for at least 10 minutes before you serve it. Or chill in refrigerator.

Nutritional Information:

- Calories: 134
- Total Fat: 7g
- Saturated Fat: 1g
- Carbohydrates: 16g
- Protein: 1g

Tomato Lime – Sunflower Seed Salad

Ingredients:
- 1 ½ Cup of Tomatoes – Diced
- 1/8 cup unshelled sunflower seeds
- 1 Cup of Green Onions – Chopped
- 1 Cup of Cucumbers – Chopped
- ¼ Cup of Lime Juice
- 1 tsp. of Grapeseed Oil
- 4 Ounces of Green Leaf Lettuce(Romaine)
- 3 Ounces of Carrots

Directions:
1. Mix all of the ingredients together, in same bowl. Leave lime juice for last.
2. Chill in refrigerator, or serve immediately.

Nutritional Information:
- Calories: 165
- Total Fat: 8g
- Saturated Fat: 1g
- Carbohydrates: 18g
- Protein: 3g

Grapefruit and Avocado Salad

Ingredients:
- 2 Grapefruits
- 1 Avocado
- 2 Tbsp. of Lime Juice
- 1 ½ tsp. of Ginger – Grated
- ½ tsp. of Salt
- ¼ tsp. of Pepper
- 1 Tbsp. of Mint
- 1 Head of Iceberg Lettuce

Directions:
1. Segment your grapefruits and then drain over your mesh strainer.
2. Reserve the juice.
3. Add ¼ cup of water.
4. Puree juice(blend), lime juice, ¼ of an avocado, ginger, pepper, and salt.
5. Pour it on the lettuce, and then toss it together.

Nutritional Information:
- Calories: 720
- Total Fat: 40g
- Saturated Fat: 1g
- Carbohydrates: 80g
- Protein: 10g

Grated Beet Salad

Ingredients:
- Juice from ½ orange
- Juice from ½ lemon
- 4 fresh beets, peeled and grated
- 2 tbsp. chopped fresh parsley
- Salt and Pepper, to taste
- Several romaine lettuce leaves

Directions:
1. Combine fruit juices and toss with beets and parsley.
2. Add salt and pepper to taste.
3. To serve, line bowl with lettuce leaves and top with beet mixture.
4. Sprinkle with additional parsley.

Nutritional Information
- Calories: 188
- Total Fat: 0 g
- Saturated Fat: 0 g
- Carbohydrates: 42 g
- Protein: 5 g

Green Bean and Tomato Salad

Ingredients:
- 4 oz. green beans
- 2 ripe, small tomatoes
- 1 garlic clove, minced
- 1 tbsp. chopped basil leaves
- 1 tbsp. vegetable juice (use water from cooking green beans)
- Pinch of salt and pinch of pepper

Directions:
1. Trim ends from green beans and cut into 1" lengths.
2. Bring a saucepan of salted water to a boil and add green beans. Cook 3-5 minutes. Add tomatoes to pan during last 10 seconds of cooking to loosen skins. Save 1 tbsp. of vegetable water from pan.
3. Peel and dice tomatoes.
4. In a bowl, combine green beans and tomatoes with garlic, basil and vegetable juice.
5. Season with salt and pepper, toss gently, and serve at immediately.

Nutritional Information
- Calories: 132
- Total Fat: 0 g
- Saturated Fat: 0 g
- Carbohydrates: 28 g
- Protein: 5 g

Zucchini – Scallion Salad

Ingredients:
- ¾ cup corn kernels
- ¾ cup julienned zucchini
- 1 scallion, sliced
- ½ tbsp. lemon juice
- ¼ cup diced radishes
- 2 tbsp. chopped fresh basil
- ¾ tsp. soy sauce.
- Pinch of black pepper
- ¼ can black beans, drained and rinsed.

Directions:
1. Combine corn, zucchini, scallions, lemon juice, soy sauce, and black pepper in a bowl. Toss well.
2. Add radishes, basil, and black beans and mix together gently.
3. Cover and refrigerate for at least an hour before serving.

Nutritional Information
- Calories: 234
- Total Fat: 2 g
- Saturated Fat: 0 g
- Carbohydrates: 50 g
- Protein: 8 g

Sweet Potato Salad

Ingredients:

- 1 cup sweet potato, peeled and cubed
- 1 apple, with skin, chopped
- 1 small red onion, chopped
- 1 tsp. fresh ginger, grated
- Seasoned rice vinegar, to taste

Directions

5. Steam sweet potatoes until soft, but not mushy. Peel. Then cube.
6. Toss all ingredients together, dress with vinegar to taste.

Nutritional Information

- Calories: 250
- Total Fat: 0.6 g
- Saturated Fat: 0 g
- Carbohydrates: 57 g
- Protein: 4 g

Pineapple Salad

Ingredients:

- ¼ cup low-fat soy vanilla yogurt
- ¼ cup crushed pineapple, drained
- 1 banana, peeled
- 1 tbsp. grape nuts(optional)
- 1 tbsp. crushed strawberries

Directions

1. Mix low-fat yogurt and pineapple together.
2. Cut banana in half, lengthwise, and place in bowl.
3. Top banana halves with yogurt mixture and sprinkle with grape nuts and top with crushed berries.

Nutritional Information

- Calories: 276.2
- Total Fat: 1.8 g
- Saturated Fat: 0g
- Carbohydrates: 61 g
- Protein: 4 g

Carrot Apple Salad

Ingredients:
- 1 carrot, grated or julienned
- 1 honey crisp apple, grated or julienned
- 2 tbsp. raisins
- 1 tsp. lemon juice
- 1 tsp. agave (optional)
- ½ tbsp. apple juice

Directions
1. Mix carrots, apples, and raisins in small serving bowl.
2. Mix agave, lemon juice, and apple juice in separate bowl. Taste to check sweetness, add more agave to make sweeter, or more lemon juice to make less sweet.
3. Pour dressing over salad and toss to coat thoroughly.
4. Serve immediately.

Nutritional Information
- Calories: 148.1
- Total Fat: 0.1 g
- Saturated Fat:0 g
- Carbohydrates: 36 g
- Protein: 0.8 g

Butter Lettuce Fruit Salad

Ingredients:

- ½ head of Butter lettuce
- ½ cup chopped pineapple, drained
- ½ tomato, diced
- 1 chopped green onion
- 1 red potato

Directions:

1. First boil the potato on the stovetop until soft. Once soft, run under cold water and then chop.
2. Tear lettuce into large mixing bowl and add pineapple and diced tomato.
3. Add potatoes and sprinkle with green onion.
4. Serve and enjoy.

Nutritional Information

- Calories: 230
- Total Fat: 1 g
- Saturated Fat: g
- Carbohydrates: 50 g
- Protein: 5 g

Kumquat-Cucumber Salad

Ingredients:
For Salad:
- ¾ cup kumquats, thinly sliced, seeds and ends discarded
- 1 small cucumber, thinly sliced

For Dressing:
- ½ cup lemon juice
- ¼ cup shredded mint leaves
- 2 tbsp. finely chopped crystallized ginger
- 2 tbsp. water.
- 2 tbsp. agave
- 1 tbsp. soy sauce

Directions:
1. To make dressing, combine all ingredients in a jar and shake well. Store any leftover dressing in a sealed container in the fridge, for up to a week.
2. In a large bowl combine the kumquats and dressing.
3. Add cucumber and toss well.
4. Serve immediately.

Nutritional Information
- Calories: 263.8
- Total Fat: 0.2 g
- Saturated Fat: 0 g
- Carbohydrates: 65 g
- Protein: 0.5 g

Plum Fruit Salad

Ingredients:

- 2 plums, pitted and sliced
- 1 peach, pitted, peeled and sliced
- ½ banana, peeled and sliced
- ¼ cup grapes
- ¼ hot pepper, seeded and cut into two pieces
- ¼ head Boston lettuce, torn into small pieces

Directions:

1. Place all the fruit in large bowl, drain any juice. Combine fruit with torn lettuce and mix well.
2. Chop pepper, and mix into fruit. (optional)

Nutritional Information

- Calories: 280.4
- Total Fat: 0.8 g
- Saturated Fat: 0 g
- Carbohydrates: 67 g
- Protein: 1.3 g

Fruit - Rice Salad

Ingredients:
- 3/4 cup cooked Jazmin rice, cooled to room temperature
- ¼ cup strawberries, quartered
- ¼ cup grape halves
- 1 kiwi fruit, sliced into quarters
- ¼ cup pineapple chunks
- ¼ cup banana slices
- 1 tbsp. pineapple juice
- 1 tbsp. low-fat soy yogurt
- ½ tbsp. agave nectar
- 2-3 lettuce leaves

Directions:
1. Combine cooked rice, strawberries, grapes, kiwi, pineapple, and bananas.
2. In a small bowl, blend or mix, pineapple juice, soy yogurt, and agave.
3. Pour "dressing" over fruit and rice mixture and toss lightly.
4. Serve on lettuce leaves.

Nutritional Information
- Calories: 297.9
- Total Fat: 1.1 g
- Saturated Fat:0 g
- Carbohydrates: 69 g
- Protein: 3 g

Honeyberry Salad

Ingredients:
- 1 cup honeydew melon balls
- 1/3 cup fresh blueberries
- 1 peach, sliced
- 3 large frozen strawberries
- ½ large frozen banana
- Fresh fruit juice as needed

Directions:
1. In a bowl, gently combine the melon balls, blueberries, and peaches, taking care not to mash the blueberries. Drain and set aside any fruit juice.
2. Place frozen strawberries and bananas in a blender or food processor with a little fresh fruit juice, ice, or water, and blend to smooth and ice-like sherbet.
3. Spoon frozen fruit sherbet over fruit salad and serve.

Nutritional Information
- Calories: 214.3
- Total Fat: 0.3 g
- Saturated Fat: g
- Carbohydrates: 50 g
- Protein: 2.9 g

Cucumber Island Salad

Ingredients:

- ½ cucumber, diced small
- ¼ green bell pepper, diced small
- 1 banana, sliced thin
- 1 orange, peeled and cut into small wedges
- ½ cup lemon soy yogurt.

Directions:

1. Place all the fruit and veggies in a large bowl.
2. Add lemon soy yogurt, mix well to combine.
3. Serve immediately.

Nutritional Information

- Calories: 371
- Total Fat: 3 g
- Saturated Fat: 0 g
- Carbohydrates: 78 g
- Protein: 8 g

Cantaloupe Salad

Ingredients:
- 1 orange
- ½ cup jicama, peeled and julienne-cut,
- ¼ cucumber, peeled and thinly sliced
- ½ cup cantaloupe, cubed and peeled
- 1 tbsp. red onion, chopped
- 1 tbsp. fresh cilantro, chopped
- ½ tbsp. fresh mint
- 1 tbsp. fresh lime juice
- Pinch Salt
- Pinch hot chili powder

Directions:
1. Peel and section oranges over a bowl; squeeze to extract juice. Set sections aside and reserve 2 tbsp. of the orange juice.
2. Place orange sections, jicama, cucumber, cantaloupe, red onion, cilantro and mint in a large bowl.
3. In a separate bowl combine orange juice, lime juice, salt and chili powder. Mix well.
4. Pour the juices over jicama mixture and toss gently.
5. Cover and chill for two hour before serving.

Nutritional Information
- Calories: 145.1
- Total Fat: 0.3 g
- Saturated Fat: 0.1 g
- Carbohydrates: 34 g
- Protein: 1.6 g

Jicama Slaw

Ingredients:
- 8 oz. shredded jicama
- 4 oz. shredded carrot
- 1 cup orange juice
- 1 cup pineapple juice
- 2 tbsp. lemon juice.
- 1 tbsp. lime juice

Directions:
1. Combine orange, pineapple, lemon and lime juice in a small saucepan and reduce on medium heat until it becomes a glaze (approximately 20 minutes).
2. Remove from heat and allow the glaze to cool for 20 minutes.
3. Combine shredded jicama and carrot in large bowl.
4. When glaze is cool to the touch, add to jicama and carrots, toss well, and serve.

Nutritional Information
- Calories: 333.8
- Total Fat: 0.2 g
- Saturated Fat: g
- Carbohydrates: 79 g
- Protein: 4 g

Melon Salad

Ingredients:

- ½ fresh mango, peeled and sliced into cubes
- ¼ cantaloupe, peeled and sliced into cubes
- ¼ honeydew, peeled and sliced into cubes
- ½ cup fresh or frozen strawberries
- ½ tbsp. lemon juice
- ½ tbsp. agave

Directions:

1. Place mango and melon pieces in a large serving bowl.
2. In a blender, blend strawberries with lemon juice and agave until smooth.
3. Drizzle sauce over fruit salad and serve immediately.

Nutritional Information

- Calories: 263.9
- Total Fat: 0.3 g
- Saturated Fat: 0 g
- Carbohydrates: 63 g
- Protein: 2.3 g

Melon Mint Salad

Ingredients:
- ½ melon (cantaloupe, honeydew, or watermelon all work)
- 2 tbsp. lime juice
- 1 tsp. agave or maple syrup
- Pinch of salt
- 3-5 mint leaves, sliced into narrow strips

Directions:
1. Cut the melon open and remove the seeds. Use a melon baller to make melon balls, or cut of the rind and cut the melon into chunks. Place melon pieces in large bowl.
2. In a separate bowl combine the lime juice and agave or maple syrup. Toss with the melon, adding a pinch of salt.
3. Garnish with mint leaves and serve immediately.

Nutritional Information
- Calories: 154.9
- Total Fat: 0.1 g
- Saturated Fat: g
- Carbohydrates: 38 g
- Protein: 0.5 g

Pear Fruit Salad

Ingredients:
For the salad:
- ¼ cup pineapple, cut into chunks
- ¼ cup pear, cut into chunks
- ½ apple, cut into chunks
- ½ banana, cut into chunks
- Kiwi, cut into chunks

For the dressing:
- 2 tbsp. orange juice
- ½ tbsp. agave (or maple) syrup
- ¼ tsp. vanilla
- Splash rosewater (optional)
- Splash orange blossom water (optional)
- Dried berries (optional)

Directions:
1. After cutting fruit into chunks, place into large bowl.
2. In a separate bowl, combine orange juice, agave syrup, vanilla, rosewater and orange blossom water.
3. Add to bowl of fruit, mix well.
4. Garnish with dried berries and serve.

Nutritional Information
- Calories: 218.2
- Total Fat: 0.2 g
- Saturated Fat: 0 g
- Carbohydrates: 53 g
- Protein: 1.1 g

Grape Cardamom Salad

Ingredients:

- 2 tbsp. white grape juice
- ½ tbsp. agave syrup
- 3 cardamom pods, split
- ¼ papaya
- ¼ mango
- ½ peach (or nectarine)
- ½ banana

Directions:

1. Put the juice, agave syrup, and cardamom pods in a small saucepan over medium-low heat and bring to just a boil. Remove from heat and allow to cool.
2. Cut the fruit into chunks. Combine all, except the banana, in a large bowl.
3. Pour the syrup concoction over the fruit, cover and chill for at least 30 minutes.
4. Stir in the banana right before serving.

Nutritional Information

- Calories: 176.3
- Total Fat: 0.3 g
- Saturated Fat: 0 g
- Carbohydrates: 46 g
- Protein: 1.4 g

Don't forget to leave me a review for this book! They are always appreciated, and I try & read them all. Thanks in advance.

I hope you enjoy these recipes. Want some more vegan recipes, that are more staple meals, that will go perfectly with many of these salads? Cool. Here are some vegan recipes, that are in some of my other recipe books. Feel free to check them out on Amazon. Enjoy!

RICE COOKER
VEGAN RECIPES
Dexter Poin
Easy Meal Prep - Easy Vegan Meals
30+ Quinoa Recipes
75+ Recipes Total

Shitake Black Bean Rice
Serves: 6
Preparation Time: 30 minutes
Ingredients

- 1 cup shitake and button mushrooms (diced)
- 1 cup long grain rice
- ½ cup cooked/or canned black beans
- One finely chopped red onion
- Three minced garlic cloves
- 1 1/2 teaspoon oil (olive or coconut)
- Two tablespoons onion powder
- 2 cups water
- ¾ tablespoon sea salt

Directions:

1. Sauté the garlic and onions in the rice cooker with some oil.
2. Add the remaining ingredients and cook for up to 25 minutes.

Nutritional Value (Amount per Serving):

- Calories 257
- Fat 5 g
- Carbohydrates 23 g
- Sugar 12 g
- Protein 13 g

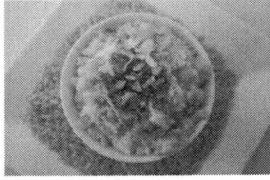

Coconut Rice with Roasted Almonds

Serves: 6

Preparation Time: 30 minutes

Ingredients

- 1 cup white rice
- 2 cups coconut milk
- ¼ cup shaved coconut (fresh)
- 8-9 almonds
- ½ teaspoon cardamom powder
- ½ tablespoon sea salt

Directions:

1. Combine all the ingredients except almonds and cover with a lid.
2. Let the rice cook for about 25 minutes. Now roast the almonds in a pan until crisp and drizzle them over the rice.

Nutritional Value (Amount per Serving):

- Calories 323
- Fat 7 g
- Carbohydrates 69 g
- Sugar 15 g
- Protein 10 g

Peanut Rice with Bell Peppers
Serves: 6
Preparation Time: 35 minutes
Ingredients
- Three finely chopped bell peppers (red, yellow and green)
- 1 cup soaked white rice
- One finely chopped red onion
- ¼ cup peanut butter
- ¼ cup tomato puree
- One teaspoon paprika powder
- One teaspoon sea salt
- 2 cups water

Directions:
1. Mix the peanut butter in some water and set aside. Now combine all the ingredients in a rice cooker and pour the peanut butter mixture over it.
2. Cook this rice for 30 minutes on medium heat.

Nutritional Value (Amount per Serving):
- Calories 368
- Fat 9 g
- Carbohydrates 63 g
- Sugar 15 g
- Protein 10 g

Lentils Kale and Miso Soup
Serves: 6
Preparation Time: 25 minutes
Ingredients
- ½ cup lentils
- 7-8 finely chopped kale leaves
- ¼ cup sweet corn
- One tablespoon of Miso paste
- One teaspoon sea salt
- One minced garlic clove
- ½ teaspoon pepper powder
- 1 cup water

Directions:
1. Combine all the ingredients and cover with a lid.
2. Cook the soup for 20 minutes.

Nutritional Value (Amount per Serving):
- Calories 256
- Fat 8 g
- Carbohydrates 45 g
- Sugar 12 g
- Protein 8 g

Apple and Raisin Porridge Rice
Serves: 6
Preparation Time: 35 minutes
Ingredients
- 1 cup rice
- One finely chopped apple
- 1 cup apple juice
- ½ teaspoon cardamom
- 7-8 raisins
- 7-8 chopped cashews
- Five tablespoons brown sugar
- 1 cup water

Directions:
1. Mix all the ingredients together along with the apple juice and cover the lid
2. Cook.

Nutritional Value (Amount per Serving):
- Calories 300
- Fat 9 g
- Carbohydrates 67 g
- Sugar 4 g
- Protein 10 g

Creamy Mushroom Soup

Serves: 6

Preparation Time: 30 minutes

Ingredients

- 1 cup diced button mushrooms
- One sliced white onion
- Two minced garlic cloves
- ¼ cup coconut milk
- ½ cup water
- One teaspoon sea salt
- ½ teaspoon pepper
- One teaspoon coconut oil

Directions:

1. Sauté the garlic, onion, mushrooms and add the rest of the ingredients to it except coconut milk.
2. Cook this soup for 20 minutes in the rice cooker. Once cooled down, blend the mixture using a hand blender.

Nutritional Value (Amount per Serving):

- Calories 368
- Fat 9 g
- Carbohydrates 63 g
- Sugar 15 g
- Protein 10 g

Spicy and Sour Sweet Potatoes
Serves: 6
Preparation Time: 10 minutes
Ingredients

- 1.5 cups peeled and diced sweet potatoes
- Two green chilies
- One tablespoon tamarind paste
- One teaspoon cumin
- 1 ½ teaspoon salt
- One bay leaf
- One teaspoon sesame seeds
- 1 cup water
- One teaspoon oil (olive or coconut)

Directions:

1. Take some oil in the rice cooker and sauté the cumin, green chilies, and sweet potatoes in it for 6 minutes.

Nutritional Value (Amount per Serving):

- Calories 236
- Fat 5 g
- Carbohydrates 25 g
- Sugar 6 g
- Protein 9 g

Lentils

Serves: 6

Preparation Time: 30 minutes

Ingredients

- ½ cup lentils
- ¼ cup spinach puree
- One finely chopped red onion
- One finely chopped tomato
- One teaspoon curry powder
- Two minced garlic cloves
- ½ teaspoon ginger paste
- One teaspoon sea salt
- 1 cup water

Directions:

1. Combine all the ingredients together and cover with a lid and cook.

Nutritional Value (Amount per Serving):

- Calories 368
- Fat 9 g
- Carbohydrates 63 g
- Sugar 15 g
- Protein 10 g

Rice Chili Stew

Serves: 6

Preparation Time: 30 minutes

Ingredients

- ½ cup rice
- ¼ cup cooked black beans
- ¼ cup sweet corn
- One minced garlic clove
- One teaspoon ginger paste
- One teaspoon cumin powder
- One teaspoon chili pepper
- One teaspoon oregano
- 1 Sliced avocado
- One teaspoon lemon juice
- 1.5 cups water

Directions:

1. Combine all ingredients in a rice cooker except avocado and lemon juice.
2. Let the stew cook for 25 minutes.
3. Sprinkle some lemon juice.

Nutritional Value (Amount per Serving):

- Calories 368
- Fat 9 g
- Carbohydrates 63 g
- Sugar 15 g
- Protein 10 g

Banana Coconut Sticky Dessert
Serves: 6
Preparation Time: 30 minutes
Ingredients

- ¾ cups sticky rice
- Two ripe bananas(sliced)
- ½ cup coconut milk
- ¼ cup shaved fresh coconut
- 1/8 cup brown sugar
- One teaspoon cardamom powder
- One teaspoon olive oil
- ½ cup almond milk

Directions:

1. In a rice cooker, add the oil along with the rest of the ingredients one by one.
2. Cook this pudding for 30-40 minutes on slow heat. Let it sit for another 15 minutes.

Nutritional Value (Amount per Serving):

- Calories 368
- Fat 9 g
- Carbohydrates 63 g
- Sugar 15 g
- Protein 10 g

Rice Cooker
VEGAN
Recipes
50 Vegan Recipes Total 20 Quinoa Recipes

Easy Meal Prep - Plant Based Cooking

Vegan

Dexter Poin

Fruit and Bean Quinoa Salad

Serves: 8

Time: 35 minutes

Ingredients:

- 1 cup quinoa
- 2 cups water
- 1 orange juice
- 1 lime juice
- 12 jalapeno pepper, minced
- 1/4 cup fresh mint, minced
- 1/4 cup fresh cilantro, minced
- 1 red bell pepper, diced
- 1 1/2 cups black beans, cooked and drained
- 1 1/2 cups avocado, peel and diced
- 2 cups mango, diced
- 2 tbsp balsamic vinegar
- 2 tbsp olive oil
- 1/2 tsp salt
- Pepper

Directions:

1. Add quinoa, water, and salt in a rice cooker. Stir well and cook for 15 minutes.
2. After 15 minutes fluff the quinoa using fork and transfer in large mixing bowl.
3. Combine together vinegar and olive oil.
4. Add vinegar and olive oil mixture to the quinoa and mix well and set aside to cool.

5. Once quinoa is cool then add orange juice, lime juice, jalapeno pepper, mint, cilantro, red bell pepper, black beans, avocado, and mangoes. Toss well.

6. Season salad with pepper and salt.

7. Serve and enjoy.

Nutritional Value (Amount per Serving):

- Calories 357
- Fat 11 g
- Carbohydrates 55 g
- Sugar 14 g
- Protein 12 g
- Cholesterol 0 mg

Cranberry Kale Quinoa

Serves: 1

Time: 25 minutes

Ingredients:

- 1/3 cup quinoa, rinsed and drained
- 2 tbsp orange juice
- 1 tbsp olive oil
- 1/3 cup cranberries, dried
- 1/2 cup kale, chopped
- 2/3 cup water
- 1/4 tsp cinnamon
- Pepper
- Salt

Directions:

1. Add quinoa, orange juice, olive oil, cranberries, kale, and water in rice cooker. Stir well.
2. Turn on rice cooker and cook quinoa for 20 minutes. Stir 2 to 3 times.
3. Once it cooks then add cinnamon, pepper, and salt. Stir well.
4. Serve and enjoy.

Nutritional Value (Amount per Serving):

- Calories 381
- Fat 17 g
- Carbohydrates 47 g
- Sugar 4 g
- Protein 9 g
- Cholesterol 0 mg

Easy Quinoa Porridge

Serves: 2

Time: 20 minutes

Ingredients:

- 1/2 cup quinoa, rinsed and drained
- 1 cup water
- 1/4 cup almonds, chopped
- 1 medium apple, diced
- 1 cup almond milk
- 1/2 cup rolled oats
- 1 tbsp maple syrup

Directions:

1. Add quinoa, oats, almond milk, and water in rice cooker and stir well.
2. Seal rice cooker with lid and cook for 15 minutes.
3. Once it cooked then open lid and stirs quinoa mixture well.
4. Add quinoa in two bowls and top with chopped almonds, apple, and maple syrup.
5. Serve warm and enjoy.

Nutritional Value (Amount per Serving):

- Calories 663
- Fat 38 g
- Carbohydrates 72 g
- Sugar 22 g
- Protein 14 g
- Cholesterol 0 mg

Simple Garlic Quinoa

Serves: 4

Time: 35 minutes

Ingredients:

- 2 cups quinoa, rinsed and drained
- 1/2 cup onion, chopped
- 1/2 tsp garlic, minced
- 1 tbsp olive oil
- 2 1/2 cups vegetable broth

Directions:

1. Add olive in the rice cooker and select sauté.
2. Add onion and garlic and sauté for 3 minutes.
3. Add quinoa and stir for 1 minute.
4. Pour vegetable broth in the rice cooker and stir well.
5. Cook quinoa in the rice cooker for 25 minutes.
6. Using fork fluff the quinoa and serve.

Nutritional Value (Amount per Serving):

- Calories 373
- Fat 9 g
- Carbohydrates 56 g
- Sugar 1 g
- Protein 15 g
- Cholesterol 0 mg

Quinoa Broccoli Casserole

Serves: 4

Time: 30 minutes

Ingredients:

- 1 1/2 cups quinoa, rinsed and drained
- 1 lemon juice
- 1 tbsp vegan butter
- 4 garlic cloves, minced
- 1 small head broccoli, chopped
- 1/4 cup vegan cheese
- 3 cups water
- Pepper
- Salt

Directions:

1. Add butter in the rice cooker and select sauté.
2. Once butter is melted then add garlic and stir for 30 seconds.
3. Add quinoa in the rice cooker and stir well.
4. Now water and lemon juice and seal cooker with lid.
5. Once the half liquid is absorbed then open the lid and stir quinoa well.
6. Add chopped broccoli on top of quinoa and cover rice cooker with lid again.
7. Once the broccoli is cooked then open the lid. Add cheese and stir well until cheese is melted.
8. Serve and enjoy.

Nutritional Value (Amount per Serving):

- Calories 290
- Fat 8 g
- Carbohydrates 44 g
- Sugar 0.4 g
- Protein 10 g
- Cholesterol 8 mg

Healthy Quinoa Salad

Serves: 6
Time: 40 minutes
Ingredients:

- For salad:
- 1/2 cup quinoa, rinsed and drained
- 2/3 cup water
- 1/4 cup vegan cheese, crumbled
- 1/2 cup cherry tomatoes, sliced
- 1/2 cup cranberries, dried
- 1/2 cup cucumbers, sliced
- 1/2 cup peas
- For dressing:
- 1 tbsp shallot, chopped
- 1 tbsp lemon juice
- 1 tsp lemon zest
- 1 tbsp vinegar
- 2 tbsp olive oil
- 1/4 tsp pepper

Directions:

1. Add water and quinoa in the rice cooker and cook on the quick cook.
2. Meanwhile, in a small bowl combine together all dressing ingredients.
3. Once quinoa is cooked then fluff with a fork and add in large mixing bowl. Set aside quinoa for 5 minutes to cool.

4. Now add tomatoes, cranberries, cucumbers, peas and cheese.

5. Pour dressing over salad and toss well.

6. Serve immediately and enjoy.

Nutritional Value (Amount per Serving):

- Calories 125
- Fat 6 g
- Carbohydrates 13 g
- Sugar 1 g
- Protein 3 g
- Cholesterol 0 mg

Blueberry Breakfast Quinoa

Serves: 4

Time: 30 minutes

Ingredients:

- 1 cup quinoa, rinsed and drained
  - 1 cup blueberries
    - 1 tsp cinnamon
    - 1/2 tsp cloves
    - 1 tsp nutmeg
    - 2 tbsp sugar
  - 1 tsp vanilla extract
- 2 cup almond milk, unsweetened

Directions:

1. Using fork mash blueberries.
2. Add all ingredients into the rice cooker and stir well.
3. Cook quinoa mixture on white rice setting.
4. Stir well and serve.

Nutritional Value (Amount per Serving):

- Calories 484
  - Fat 31 g
- Carbohydrates 46 g
  - Sugar 13 g
  - Protein 9 g
- Cholesterol 0 mg

Green Beans Quinoa

Serves: 4

Time: 30 minutes

Ingredients:

- 1 cup quinoa, rinsed and drained
- 1 1/3 cup water
- 1/2 cup cashews, roasted
- 3 tbsp vinaigrette
- 1 medium tomato, cored and chopped
- 12 oz green beans, remove stems and chopped
- 1 tsp salt

Directions:

1. Add quinoa, salt, and water in rice cooker. Stir well and start rice cooker on white rice setting.
2. Once quinoa starts boiling then add green beans on steamer rack and place steamer over quinoa.
3. Cover and cook green beans for 5 minutes.
4. After 5 minutes remove steamer and cook quinoa continue for total 15 minutes.
5. Using fork fluff the quinoa and place in large mixing bowl.
6. Add chopped tomatoes, steamed green beans, and vinaigrette in quinoa and toss well.
7. Top quinoa with cashews and serve.

Nutritional Value (Amount per Serving):

- Calories 341
- Fat 16 g
- Carbohydrates 40 g
- Sugar 3 g
- Protein 10 g
- Cholesterol 0 mg

Tasty Red Quinoa with Rice

Serves: 4

Time: 30 minutes

Ingredients:

- 1/2 cup red quinoa, rinsed and drained
- 3 cups water
- 1 cup rice, rinsed and drained
- 1 tbsp olive oil
- 1/4 tsp salt

Directions:

1. Add all ingredients into the rice cooker and stir well.
2. Start rice cooker.
3. Once rice cooker rice setting changes to warm then open the lid.
4. Stir well and serve.

Nutritional Value (Amount per Serving):

- Calories 284
- Fat 4 g
- Carbohydrates 54 g
- Sugar 0.6 g
- Protein 5 g
- Cholesterol 0 mg

Kale Raisin Quinoa

Serves: 1

Time: 30 minutes

Ingredients:

- 1/3 cup quinoa, rinsed and drained
- 1 cup kale, chopped
- 1/4 cup almond milk
- 1/2 tsp cinnamon
- 3 tbsp raisins
- 2/3 cup water
- 1/4 tsp salt

Directions:

1. Add quinoa, water, salt, cinnamon, and raisins in the rice cooker and stir well.
2. Start rice cooker. When rice cooker goes on warm mode then open the lid and stir well.
3. Add kale and almond milk and stir well and set it in warm mode for 5 minutes.
4. Serve and enjoy.

Nutritional Value (Amount per Serving):

- Calories 464
- Fat 17 g
- Carbohydrates 69 g
- Sugar 18 g
- Protein 12 g
- Cholesterol 0 mg

Mixed Vegetable Quinoa

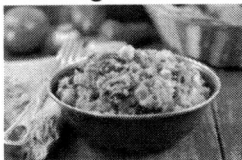

Serves: 4
Time: 30 minutes
Ingredients:

- 1 cup quinoa, rinsed and drained
- 2 tbsp liquid amino
- 1 tbsp sesame oil
- 2 cup mixed vegetables
- 3 cups vegetable broth

Directions:

1. Add vegetable broth and quinoa in the rice cooker and stir well.
2. Add vegetables to steamer basket and place over quinoa.
3. Cook quinoa on white rice setting. It takes 20 minutes to cook.
4. Once cooking finish then adds quinoa and vegetable in large mixing bowl.
5. Add liquid amino and sesame oil in quinoa and vegetable mixture and stir well.
6. Serve warm and enjoy.

Nutritional Value (Amount per Serving):

- Calories 259
- Fat 7 g
- Carbohydrates 37 g
- Sugar 0.5 g
- Protein 12 g
- Cholesterol 0 mg

RAW FOOD
RECIPES

Dexter Poin

50 Unique & Delicious Raw Food Recipes
Vegan & Vegetarian Approved!

Raw Hot Chocolate

Total Time: 10 minutes
Servings: 1 (Serving Size: 8-10 fl.oz.)

Ingredients

½ c. cashews
3 medjool dates, pitted
3 tsp. cacao powder
pinch vanilla bean powder
1 cup water
1 strawberry, to garnish

Directions

Place all of the ingredients, except for the strawberry into a blender; process on high for 1-2 minutes or until smooth and beginning to heat up a bit.

Pour into a large mug and garnish with a strawberry, Drink right away and enjoy!

Whipped Strawberry-Coconut Smoothie

Total Time: 10 minutes
Servings: 2 (Serving Size: 8 fl. oz.)

Ingredients

4 c. fresh strawberries, hulled
2 c. raw coconut milk
1 medium pear, chopped
1 orange, peeled and sectioned
5 to 6 ice cubes
4 tbsp. shaved coconut meat, to garnish

Directions

Prepare ingredients as directed and then combine the ingredients in the order listed into the blender.

Begin blending on low speed and then gradually increase speed to blend on high, continue blending 30-60 seconds or until smooth.

Pour smoothie into serving glasses and garnish with shaved pieces of coconut meat. Drink immediately to receive full nutritional value. Any remaining smoothie can be refrigerated for up 48 hours, in an airtight, opaque container as to not be exposed to light, heat, or air due to risk of oxidation and loss of nutrients.

Coconut Mint-Chip Shake

Total Time: 10 minutes
Servings: 2 (Serving Size: 8 fl. oz.)

Ingredients

½ c. full-fat coconut milk
½ c. raw coconut meat, chopped
½ c. packed raw spinach
2 tbsp. packed mint leaves
1-2 drops peppermint extract
1 c. ice cubes
1 avocado, peeled and chopped
honey, to taste
2 tsp. cacao nibs

Directions

In a blender, combine the coconut milk, coconut meat, spinach, mint, avocado, and ice until smooth and frothy. Taste and add in the peppermint extract, if needed.

Finally, add in the honey and cacao nibs. Blend again very briefly breaking down the nibs into little bits.

Pour into 2 glasses, garnish with a sprig of mint and a few chopped cacao nibs. Drink immediately.

Stuffed Apricots with Cashew Chevre

Total Time: 20 minutes
Servings: 4 (Serving Size: 1 crepe with filling)

Ingredients

14 ripe organic apricots
1½ c. Organic cashews
½ c. filtered water
½ tsp. raw organic apple cider vinegar
1 medium ripe organic lemon
2 tbsp. fresh organic edible lavender flowers/petals, chopped fine
1 tbsp. fresh organic edible lavender leaves, chopped fine

Directions

Prepare the Cashew Chevre: In the bowl of a food processor, add the cashews and grind them into a fine powder. Transfer the ground cashew powder to a medium-sized mixing bowl and stir in the water until well blended.

Let rest at room temperature for 15 minutes. Then stir in the vinegar and let rest an additional 15 minutes. Next, add in the lemon juice and lemon zest, stir well to incorporate, then set aside.

Prepare the Apricots by rinsing in cool running water, then patting dry with paper towel. Next, cut each apricot in half lengthwise and remove the stones from each. Discard stones.

Finely dice up two whole apricots and add it to the bowl with the cashew mixture and stir to incorporate. Next, add in 1 tbsp. of the chopped lavender flowers as well as all of the chopped leaves. Blend well.

Using a melon baller, spoon a melon ball-size scoop of flesh out of the center of each of the apricot halves. Take care to not pierce the outer skin. Place all of the scooped apricot flesh onto a cutting board and chop it up very finely. Set aside to use as garnish.

Assemble the Stuffed Apricots: Using the melon baller, get a heaping scoop of the cashew chevre mixture and place it into the hollowed-out part of one of the apricot halves. Set the stuffed apricot onto a platter and repeat to stuff the remaining apricot halves.

When all of the apricot halves are stuffed, garnish the stuffed apricots with the chopped apricot and the remaining chopped lavender flowers/petals.

To serve, place 2 stuffed apricots on each plate and enjoy!

Chia Seed Oatmeal with Cinnamon Mixed Berries

Total Time: 30 minutes
Servings: 1 (Serving Size: 1 bowl oatmeal)

Ingredients

4 tbsp. of chia seeds
1 c. almond milk (or soy/nut milk of choice)
1 tbsp. raw honey
¼ c. unsweetened flaked coconut
1 c. mixed fresh raspberries and blackberries
1-2 tsp. ground cinnamon

Directions

Place the chia seeds in a large serving bowl with the almond milk (or coconut milk). Stir to combine. Add honey, stir again to combine, and then let rest at room temperature for 10-20 minutes or until the chia seeds absorb the liquid and soften and expand.

When the chia seed oatmeal is nearly done, place the mixed berries in a separate bowl. Sprinkle the berries with the cinnamon and toss to coat.

When the oatmeal is ready, garnish the surface of the oatmeal with flaked coconut and the mixed berries. Serve immediately.

Pecan Sandies

Total Time: 10 hours and 20 minutes (Includes about 10 hours dehydrating time)
Servings: 12 (Serving Size: 2 cookies)

Ingredients

3 c. raw pecans, divided to yield 1 ½ c. ground pecans and 24 whole pecan halves

1¾ c. dried unsweetened flaked coconut
¾ c. maple syrup
1/3 c. coconut oil, softened
1 tsp. vanilla extract (or 1 vanilla bean, scraped, if preferred)
1 tsp. almond extract (opt.)
½ tsp. sea salt, or to taste

Directions

Take out 24 pecan halves out of the 3 cups of raw pecans; set them aside until needed. Place the remaining pecans in a food processor. Pulse until they are ground and measure out to yield 1½ c. of the ground pecans; set aside until needed.

In a large mixing bowl combine the flaked coconut, the reserved 1½ c. ground pecans, maple syrup, softened coconut oil, vanilla extract (or scraped vanilla bean), almond extract (opt.), and ½ tsp. sea salt, or to taste. Mix until well combined.

Take 1 tbsp. of the mixture into your hand and form it into a ball, place the ball of dough onto a non-stick dehydrator sheet, and press down and flatten slightly with the back of a tablespoon.

Press 1 of the pecan halves in the center of the flattened ball and press it lightly into the dough. Repeat with remaining dough and pecan halves to make the remaining 23 cookies. Use multiple non-stick dehydrating sheets, if needed.

Dehydrate the pecan sandies at 115°F for 12-24 hours or until done. Yield: 24 Pecan Sandies.

Come hang out with me on Instagram - **@dextersworld**

Chocolate Ice Cream

Total Time: 2 hours 10 minutes (includes about 2 hours freezing time)

Servings: 4 (Serving Size: ½ c.)

Ingredients

1¾ c. cashews, coarsely chopped
1¾ c. purified water
1 c. maple syrup
2 tsp. vanilla extract
¼ tsp. almond extract
½ c. unsweetened cocoa powder

Directions

In a blender, combine the coarsely chopped cashews, purified water, maple syrup, vanilla extract, almond extract, and cocoa powder. Process until well combined.

If using an ice cream maker, pour the mixture into the ice cream maker and process/freeze according to manufacturer directions.

If you do not own an ice cream maker, pour the mixture into an airtight container and freeze it for about 2 hours, just as you would regular ice cream.

Once frozen, serve and enjoy! Yield: 2 cups.

Cantaloupe Dessert Soup with Coconut Milk

Total Time: 1 hour 20 minutes
Servings: 4 (Serving Size: 1 cup)

Ingredients

3 c. cantaloupe, diced
1½ c. coconut milk
2 tbsp. raw honey
Juice from 1 lime
2 – 3 fresh basil leaves, chopped
½ tsp. cinnamon
¼ tsp. ginger
Pinch of sea salt, or to taste
Basil leaves, for garnish (opt.)

Directions

Prepare ingredients as directed then combine the ingredients in the order listed together in your blender.

Blend on medium-high speed for 20-30 seconds or until smooth. Taste and adjust, if needed, by adding more cantaloupe, coconut milk, cinnamon, or honey. Blend for 5-10 seconds more to fully incorporate then transfer contents to a pitcher.

Place in refrigerator to chill for 1 hour.

When ready to serve, pour into dessert bowls and garnish with fresh parsley (opt.). Always serve chilled!

Falafels with Fava Beans

Total Time: 1 hour 15 minutes
Servings: 2-3 (Serving Size: 2 patties)

Ingredients

1 tsp. tahini
1 carrot, grated
2 c. fresh fava beans, peeled
Juice from ½ a lemon
2 spring onions, chopped
1 tsp. sea salt, or to taste
1 fresh clove garlic, minced
½ c. sesame seeds

Directions

Begin by peeling the fava beans and then placing them in a blender or food processor along with the tahini, grated carrot, lemon juice, chopped spring onion, sea salt, and the minced garlic. Process until well blended.

Place the sesame seeds in a shallow bowl.

With wet hands, shape the mixture into small patties. You should have enough batter to create 4-6 patties.

Dredge the patties through the sesame seeds to coat, place on a plate, and chill in the refrigerator for 1 hour.
To serve, place in a serving dish garnished with fresh parsley, if desired. Be sure to always serve these falafels chilled!

VEGAN
Smoothie
Recipes 1

Anti - Inflammatory
Immune Boosting

Dexter Poin

Creamy Green Avocado Cucumber Smoothie

Total Time: 5 minutes

Serves: 4

Ingredients:

- 1 avocado, remove seed and scoop out
- 1/2 cup filtered water
- 1 lime juice
- Cilantro – to preference
- 1 small cucumber, peel and remove seeds

Directions:

1. Add all ingredients into the blender and blend until smooth.

Nutritional Value (Amount per Serving):

- Calories 109
- Fat 9.8 g
- Carbohydrates 5.8 g
- Sugar 0.9 g
- Protein 1.2 g
- Cholesterol 0 mg

Fig Smoothie

Total Time: 5 minutes

Serves: 2

Ingredients:

- 4 fresh figs
- 1 tbsp flax seeds
- 1 medium banana
- 1 1/2 cup almond milk
- ¼ cup oats
- 1 tsp cinnamon

Directions:

1. Add all ingredients into the blender and blend until smooth.

Nutritional Value (Amount per Serving):

- Calories 631
- Fat 45.4 g
- Carbohydrates 58.3 g
- Sugar 31.6 g
- Protein 8.4 g
- Cholesterol 0 mg

Cantaloupe and Peach Smoothie

Total Time: 5 minutes

Serves: 4

Ingredients:

- 2 cups cantaloupe
  - 1 cup ice
  - 1/2 tbsp Stevia
  - 1 cup orange juice
  - 8 slices of peaches

Directions:

1. Add all ingredients into the blender and blend until smooth.

Nutritional Value (Amount per Serving):

- Calories 231
  - Fat 1.9 g
- Carbohydrates 48.0 g
  - Sugar 46.5 g
  - Protein 7.9 g
  - Cholesterol 4 mg

Green Kale and Kiwi Smoothie

Total Time: 5 minutes

Serves: 2

Ingredients:

- 1 cup kale, washed
- 2 kiwi, peeled and sliced
- 1/2 cup ice cube
- 2 tbsp stevia
- 1 cup almond milk
- 2 ripe bananas

Directions:

1. Add all ingredients into the blender and blend until smooth.

2. Serve immediately and enjoy.

Nutritional Value (Amount per Serving):

- Calories 293
- Fat 3.3 g
- Carbohydrates 64.9 g
- Sugar 44.0 g
- Protein 7.2 g
- Cholesterol 10 mg

Mango Strawberry Smoothie

Total Time: 5 minutes

Serves: 3

Ingredients:

- 1 cup mango, diced
- 1 cup almond milk
- 1 cup strawberries
- 1 ripe banana

Directions:

1. Add all ingredients into the blender and blend until smooth and creamy.

Nutritional Value (Amount per Serving):

- Calories 158
- Fat 2.4 g
- Carbohydrates 33.3 g
- Sugar 26.2 g
- Protein 4.3 g
- Cholesterol 7 mg

Pineapple Avocado Smoothie

Total Time: 5 minutes
Serves: 4
Ingredients:

- 2 cups pineapple, cut into chunks
- 2 avocados, remove seed and scoop out
- 1 cup almond milk
- 1 large banana
- 2 cups chopped spinach
- 1 cup pineapple juice

Directions:

1. Add all ingredients into the blender and blend until smooth.

Nutritional Value (Amount per Serving):

- Calories 451
- Fat 34.2 g
- Carbohydrates 39.1 g
- Sugar 21.1 g
- Protein 4.8 g
- Cholesterol 0 mg

Pineapple Orange Smoothie

Total Time: 5 minutes
Serves: 2
Ingredients:
- 1/2 cup pineapple chunks
- 4 tbsp coconut milk
- 3/4 cup fresh orange juice
- 6 tbsp vanilla vegan ice cream
- 1/2 tbsp ground flax seed
- 1 banana

Directions:
1. Add all ingredients into the blender and blend until smooth.

Nutritional Value (Amount per Serving):
- Calories 200
- Fat 8.6 g
- Carbohydrates 27.2 g
- Sugar 19.7 g
- Protein 4.5 g
- Cholesterol 3 mg

Kale Banana Smoothie

Total Time: 5 minutes

Serves: 2

Ingredients:

- 2 cups kale, remove stems
- 1 banana
- 2 cups water
- 2 tbsp chia seeds
- 1/2 lime juice
- 2 cups pineapple chunks

Directions:

1. Add kale and water in blender and blend until smooth.
2. Now add remaining ingredients into the blender and blend again until smooth.
3. Serve immediately and enjoy.

Nutritional Value (Amount per Serving):

- Calories 168
- Fat 0.4 g
- Carbohydrates 42.1 g
- Sugar 23.5 g
- Protein 3.5 g

Watermelon Strawberry Smoothie

Total Time: 5 minutes

Serves: 4

Ingredients:

- 4 cups watermelon chunks
  - 2 cups strawberry
    - 1 inch ginger
  - 2 tbsp chia seeds
  - 2 tbsp lime juice

Directions:

1. Add all ingredients into the blender and blend until smooth.

Nutritional Value (Amount per Serving):

- Calories 70
  - Fat 0.5 g
- Carbohydrates 16.9 g
  - Sugar 12.9 g
  - Protein 1.4 g
- Cholesterol 0 mg

Energy Lime Watermelon Smoothie

Total Time: 5 minutes

Serves: 2

Ingredients:

- 1 tbsp lime juice
- 2 cups watermelon chunks
- 3 fresh mint leaves
- 2 cups fresh strawberries

Directions:

1. Add all ingredients into the blender and blend until smooth.
2. Serve immediately and enjoy.

Nutritional Value (Amount per Serving):

- Calories 92
- Fat 0.6 g
- Carbohydrates 22.5 g
- Sugar 16.4 g
- Protein 1.9 g
- Cholesterol 0 mg

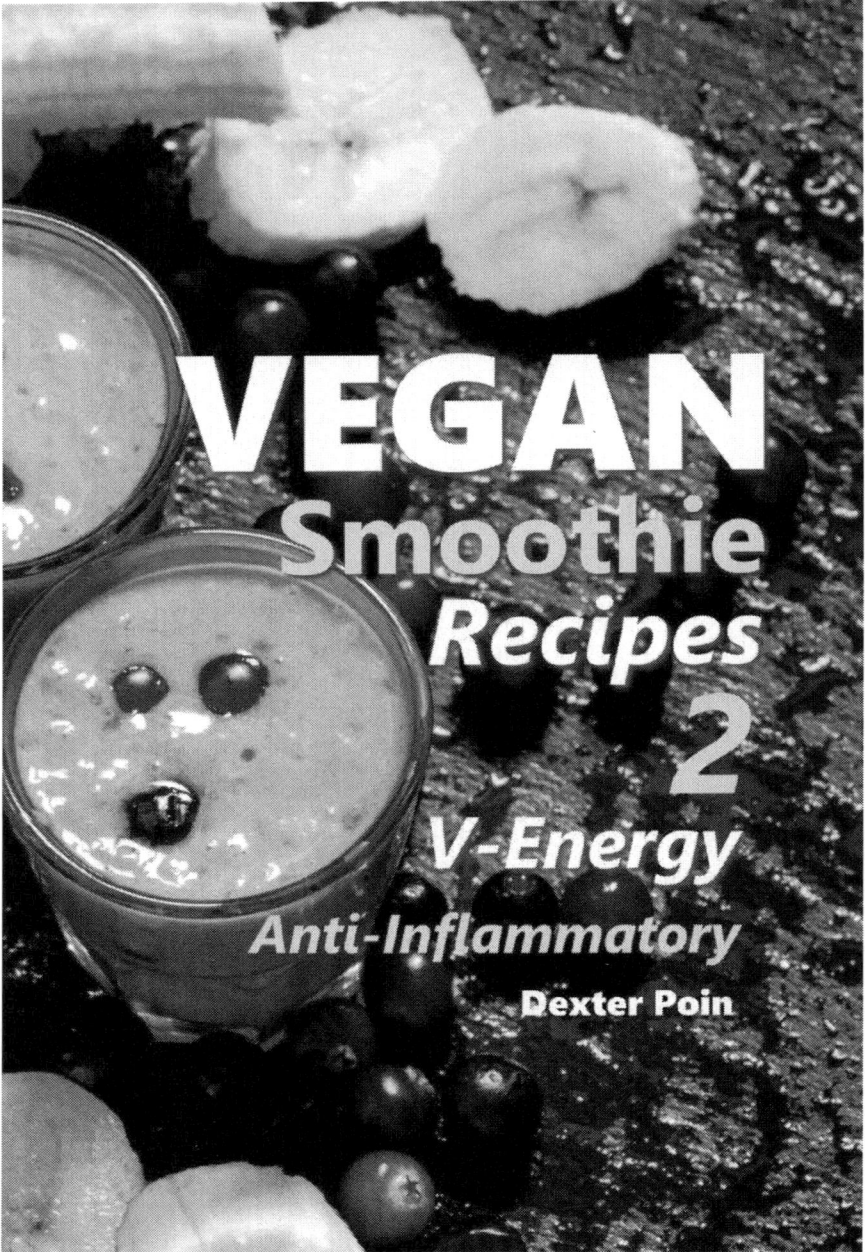

VEGAN
Smoothie
Recipes
2

V-Energy
Anti-Inflammatory

Dexter Poin

Apple Beet Smoothie

Total Time: 8 minutes

Serves: 4

Ingredients:

- 2 gala apple, diced
- 1 small beet, diced
- 1 cup filtered water
- 1 cup orange juice
- 12 ice cubes
- 1 1/2 cups fresh strawberries
- 3 tsp lemon juice
- 2 medium bananas

Directions:

1. Add all ingredients into the blender and blend until smooth.

Nutritional Value (Amount per Serving):

- Calories 145
- Fat 0.8 g
- Carbohydrates 34.7 g
- Sugar 24.1 g
- Protein 2.0 g

Choco Cherry Smoothie

Total Time: 5 minutes
Serves: 2
Ingredients:

- 4 tbsp cocoa powder, unsweetened
- 2 cups cherries
- 2 cups almond milk, unsweetened
- 2 tbsp chia seeds
- 1/2 cup rolled oats
- 2 dates

Directions:

1. Add all ingredients into the blender and blend until smooth and creamy.

Nutritional Value (Amount per Serving):

- Calories 748
- Fat 60.7 g
- Carbohydrates 56.4 g
- Sugar 27.6 g
- Protein 11.8 g

Melon Mint Smoothie

Total Time: 5 minutes
Serves: 2
Ingredients:

- 3 cups ripe honeydew melon
  - 2 cup ice
  - 20 mint leaves
  - 5 tbsp lemon juice
- 1 1/3 cup plain vegan yogurt

Directions:

1. Add all ingredients into the blender and blend until smooth and creamy.

2. Serve and enjoy.

Nutritional Value (Amount per Serving):

- Calories 249
- Fat 2.7 g
- Carbohydrates 44.1 g
- Sugar 41.6 g
- Protein 11.0 g

Zinger Ginger Honeydew Smoothie

Total Time: 5 minutes

Serves: 2

Ingredients:

- 1 cup honeydew melon
  - 1 inch ginger
  - 1 ripe banana
  - 1 cup watermelon
  - 1 cup cantaloupe
  - 1 cup almond milk

Directions:

1. Add all ingredients into the blender and blend until smooth.

Nutritional Value (Amount per Serving):

- Calories 408
  - Fat 29.2 g
- Carbohydrates 39.9 g
  - Sugar 28.9 g
  - Protein 5.0 g

Guava Smoothie

Total Time: 5 minutes
Serves: 2
Ingredients:
- 1 guava, sliced
- 4 tbsp coconut milk
- 1 cup fresh raspberries
- 1 cup pomegranate seeds
- 1/4 cup ice cubes

Directions:
1. Add all ingredients into the blender and blend until smooth.
2. Serve immediately and enjoy.

Nutritional Value (Amount per Serving):
- Calories 132
- Fat 8.0 g
- Carbohydrates 15.4 g
- Sugar 7.7 g
- Protein 2.6 g

Cranberry Banana Smoothie

Total Time: 5 minutes

Serves: 2

Ingredients:

- 1 cup cranberries
  - 1 banana
  - 1 orange
- 1 cup almond milk, unsweetened
  - 6 ice cubes

Directions:

1. Add all ingredients into the blender and blend until smooth and creamy.

Nutritional Value (Amount per Serving):

- Calories 402
  - Fat 28.9 g
- Carbohydrates 35.9 g
  - Sugar 21.8 g
  - Protein 4.2 g

Apricot Berries Smoothie

Total Time: 5 minutes
Serves: 2
Ingredients:

- 2 apricots, pitted
- 1 cup almond milk
- 1 cup mix berries
- 1 cup ice cubes

Directions:

1. Add all ingredients into the blender and blend until smooth and creamy.
2. Serve immediately and enjoy.

Nutritional Value (Amount per Serving):

- Calories 365
- Fat 29.1 g
- Carbohydrates 27.6 g
- Sugar 20.8 g
- Protein 3.7 g

Sweet Potato Ginger Smoothie

Total Time: 5 minutes

Serves: 2

Ingredients:

- 1 sweet potato
- 1 inch fresh ginger
- 2 carrots
- 1/2 cup pineapple chunks

Directions:

1. Add all ingredients into the blender and blend until smooth.

Nutritional Value (Amount per Serving):

- Calories 97
- Fat 0.3 g
- Carbohydrates 23.2 g
- Sugar 10.8 g
- Protein 1.9 g

Cucumber Ginger Smoothie

Total Time: 5 minutes
Serves: 2
Ingredients:

- 1/2 fennel
- 1 large cucumber
- 1 inch fresh ginger
- 1/4 lemon juice
- 2 green apples
- 4 celery ribs

Directions:

1. Add all ingredients into the blender and blend until smooth.

Nutritional Value (Amount per Serving):

- Calories 139
- Fat 0.6 g
- Carbohydrates 36.3 g
- Sugar 25.7 g
- Protein 1.6 g

Apple Peanut Butter Smoothie

Total Time: 5 minutes

Serves: 4

Ingredients:

- 2 medium apples, diced
- 2 tbsp peanut butter
- 2 cups ice cubes
- 1 tsp cinnamon

Directions:

1. Add apple, peanut butter and ice cubes into the blender and blend until smooth and creamy.
2. Pour into the glasses and sprinkle with cinnamon on top.

Nutritional Value (Amount per Serving):

- Calories 106
- Fat 4.2 g
- Carbohydrates 17.4 g
- Sugar 12.4 g
- Protein 2.3 g

Chocolate Avocado Smoothie

Total Time: 5 minutes
Serves: 2
Ingredients:

- 1/2 avocado, remove seed and scoop out
- 2 tbsp cocoa powder
- 1 1/2 cups almond milk, unsweetened
- 3 tbsp peanut butter
- 1 medium ripe banana

Directions:

1. Add all ingredients into the blender and blend until smooth and creamy.

Nutritional Value (Amount per Serving):

- Calories 738
- Fat 65.7 g
- Carbohydrates 39.8 g
- Sugar 20.1 g
- Protein 12.7 g

Mango Avocado Smoothie

Total Time: 5 minutes

Serves: 4

Ingredients:

- 2 cups mango
- 1 avocado, remove seed and scoop out
- 2 cups almond milk
- 1 cup plain vegan yogurt

Directions:

1. Add all ingredients into the blender and blend until smooth and creamy.

Nutritional Value (Amount per Serving):

- Calories 539
- Fat 39.8 g
- Carbohydrates 44.6 g
- Sugar 35.9 g
- Protein 8.6 g

VEGAN

Recipes

50

Eat Clean - Get Lean
Train Mean - But Be Nice

Dexter Poin

Creamy Wild Rice Chowder

Ingredients:

- ¼ cup raw cashews, soaked overnight and drained
- ½ medium potato, cooked with skin
- ½ can white beans, rinsed
- 1 tsp. extra-virgin olive oil
- ½ yellow onion, diced
- 2 cloves garlic, minced
- ½ rib celery, diced
- ¼ cup wild rice, not cooked
- ¼ cup brown rice, soaked overnight and drained
- 2 cups vegetable broth (or water)
- ¼ Tbsp. white or yellow miso paste
- 1 Tbsp. white balsamic vinegar (or ½ Tbsp. lemon juice)
- ¼ cup white wine (optional)
- Salt & Pepper, to taste
- ¼ cup fresh parsley, chopped

Directions:

1. Combine cashews, cooked potato, and white beans in a food processor or blender and blend well until completely smooth. If needed, add a little of the water or vegetable broth to blend.

2. Heat oil in a large saucepan or small pot over medium heat. Add the onion, garlic, and celery and a pinch of salt. Stir and continue cooking until soft, about 3-5 minutes.

3.   Add the wild rice and brown rice. Stir and cook for another
1-2 minutes
4.   Add the vegetable broth and bring the mixture to a boil.
Once it boils, reduce the heat to medium.
5.   Whisk the miso with a bit of water to thin it out. Add the
miso, vinegar, white wine and a pinch of pepper.
6.   Stir in the cashew mixture and continue to cook the soup at
a steady simmer, stirring frequently to ensure the rice does not
stick to the bottom. Add more broth if you would like a thinner
chowder.
7.   Simmer for 30-45 minutes (until the wild rice is cooked).
8.   Season with salt and pepper and top with parsley. Any extra
can be stored in an airtight container, in the fridge, for up to a
week.

Nutritional Information (for one serving, approximately 1/4th of
soup)
- Calories: 175.1
- Total Fat: 4.3g
- Saturated Fat: 0.9g
- Carbohydrates: 28.7g
- Protein: 5.4g

Vegan Bean Burger

Ingredients:

- 1 Tbsp. onion, diced
- 1 Tbsp. grated carrot
- 1 Tbsp. bread crumbs
- 1/4 cup kidney beans, rinsed and drained
- ¼ cup cannellini beans, rinsed and drained
- ½ Tbsp. parsley, finely chopped
- Pinch of chili powder
- Salt and Pepper to taste
- 1 tsp. flour
- 3 Tbsp. Extra Virgin Olive Oil for frying
- Whole wheat hamburger bun

Directions:

1. Put half the breadcrumbs in a mixing bowl.
2. Heat 1 Tbsp. olive oil in a medium saucepan and add onion. Cook for 3 minutes, or until softened and then add the grated carrot and cook for an additional 2-3 minutes. Add onions and carrots the breadcrumbs.
3. In a separate bowl, roughly mash the kidney and cannellini beans with a fork and then stir into the carrot mixture. Add a pinch of chili powder, salt and pepper.
4. In a shallow bowl, combine the remaining breadcrumbs with flour, parsley, salt, and pepper.
5. Shape your bean-carrot blend into 1 or 2 burger patties. Thoroughly coat the patty in the flour mixture.

6.   Heat 2 Tbsp. olive oil in a frying pan over medium heat. Carefully add your burger patty and fry each side until golden brown (about 5 minutes).

7.   Place in whole wheat bun, top with desired condiments, and enjoy.

Nutritional Information
- Calories: 225.2
- Total Fat: 1.6g
- Saturated Fat: 0.2g
- Carbohydrates: 44.7g
- Protein: 8g

Swiss Chard with Garbanzo Beans and Couscous

Ingredients:
- 4 Tbsp. couscous
- 2 Tbsp. pine nuts
- 1 Tbsp. Extra Virgin Olive Oil
- 1 clove garlic, thinly sliced
- 5 Tbsp. garbanzo beans, drained and rinsed
- 2 Tbsp. golden raisins (or dark)
- ½ bunch Swiss Chard, stems trimmed
- Salt and Pepper, to taste

Directions:

1. Place the couscous in a large bowl and add 1/3 cup boil water. Stir, cover tightly and let stand for 10 minutes.
2. While the couscous cooks, toast the pine nuts in a large skillet over low heat. Toast for 3-4 minutes, shaking the pan frequently. Set toasted pine nuts aside.
3. Heat olive oil in the skillet over medium heat. Add the garlic and cook until fragrant, about 1 minute.
4. Add the garbanzo beans, raisins, chard, salt and pepper. Cook for about 5 minutes, stirring occasionally, until chard is tender. Remove from heat.
5. Fluff couscous with a fork and place in a bowl or plate. Top with prepared chard, sprinkle with pine nuts, and enjoy.

Nutritional Information
- Calories: 142.4
- Total Fat: 6 g
- Saturated Fat: 0.25 g
- Carbohydrates: 17.8 g
- Protein: 4.3 g

Garbanzo Curry

Ingredients:

- ¾ tsp. extra-virgin olive oil
- ¼ onion, minced
- ½ clove garlic, minced
- ¼ tsp. fresh ginger root, finely chopped
- 1 whole clove
- 1/8 tsp. cinnamon
- 1/8 tsp. ground cumin
- 1/8 tsp ground coriander.
- Pinch of salt
- 1/8 tsp. cayenne pepper
- 1/8 tsp. ground turmeric
- ¼ 15oz-can garbanzo beans, drained and rinsed.
- 2 Tbsp. chopped fresh cilantro
- 1/4 cup jasmine rice
- 1/2 cup water

Directions:

1. First prepare the rice by placing both the rice and water in a medium saucepan or small pot. Turn the heat to high until it begins to boil, and then reduce to low, cover and let simmer for 15 minutes.

2. Heat olive oil in a large frying pan over medium heat for 1 minute. Sauté onions until tender, about 3-4 minutes.

3. Stir in garlic, ginger, clove, cinnamon, cumin, coriander, salt, cayenne, and turmeric. Cook for 1 minute over medium heat, stirring constantly.

4. Add in garbanzo beans and a little bit of water (about ½ Tbsp.).

5. Continue to cook for, stirring occasionally, for about 15-20 minutes, or until all the ingredients are well-blended and cooked through. Remove from heat.

6. Place cooked rice in a bowl, top with garbanzo curry, and garnish with cilantro.

Nutritional Information
- Calories: 294.9
- Total Fat: 4.5g
- Carbohydrates: 56.5g
- Protein: 7.1g

Vegan Polenta Arepas

Ingredients:

- 1/4 (8 oz.) container of tofu, drained
- 1/4 (16oz) tube prepared polenta
- 1/2 Tbsp. Extra virgin olive oil
- 1/2 banana, sliced lengthwise
- 1/4 cup black beans, undrained
- 1/2 avocado, sliced thinly
- 1/4 mango, diced
- 1 Tbsp. diced onion
- 1/4 jalapeno, seeded and diced
- Salt and pepper, to taste

Directions:

1. Preheat the oven's broiler and set the oven rack about 6 inches from the heat source.
2. Slice the tofu and polenta into equal-sized slabs, brush with olive oil and arrange on a greased baking sheet.
3. Cook the tofu and polenta under the broiler until the tops are crispy, about 5 minutes. Remove from onion and set aside.
4. Heat the olive oil in medium skillet over medium-high heat. Sauté the bananas until crispy on the outside, about 5 minutes. Remove from oil and set aside.
5. Place the black beans into a blender and blend until it becomes a thick sauce.

6. In a separate bowl, combine mango, onion, jalapeno, salt and pepper.
7. To arrange, place a slice of polenta on a plate and top with 1/4 of the bean sauce, then tofu, banana, avocado, and then top with the mango salsa and serve.

Nutritional Information
- Calories: 409.9
- Total Fat: 15.5 g
- Saturated Fat: 4.6 g
- Carbohydrates: 54 g
- Protein: 13.6 g

Ginger Stir-Fry with Coconut Rice

Ingredients:

- 1/2 tsp. corn starch
- 1/2 clove garlic, crushed
- 1/2 tsp. chopped fresh ginger root, divided
- 2 tsp. extra virgin olive-oil, divided
- 1/4 cup broccoli florets
- 1 Tbsp. snow peas
- 2 Tbsp. julienned carrots
- 1 Tbsp. red bell pepper, diced
- 1 tsp. soy sauce
- 1 tsp. water
- 1/2 Tbsp. chopped onion
- 1/4 cup jasmine rice
- 1/4 cup coconut milk
- 1/4 cup water
- Sriracha (or other hot sauce)

Directions:

1.   First prepare the rice by placing the rice, coconut milk, and water in a medium saucepan or small pot. Turn the heat to high until it begins to boil, and then reduce to low, cover and let simmer for 15 minutes, or until most of the coconut milk has been absorbed.

2.   In a large bowl, blend cornstarch, garlic, half the ginger, and 1 tsp. olive oil until cornstarch is dissolved.

3.   Add the broccoli, snow peas, carrots, and bell pepper, tossing to lighting coat.

4.   Heat the remaining olive oil in a wok over medium heat. Add vegetables, cook for 1 minute, stirring constantly to prevent burning.

5.   Add onions, salt, remaining ginger, soy sauce and water. Cook until vegetables are tender, but still crisp—about 2 minutes.

6.   Place coconut rice in a bowl, top with ginger stir fry. Add Sriracha to taste.

Nutritional Information

- Calories: 338.6
- Total Fat: 16.2 g
- Carbohydrates: 42 g
- Protein: 6.2 g

Avocado Tacos

Ingredients:

- 1 avocado, peeled, pitted, and mashed
- 2 Tbsp. onions, diced
- 1/8 tsp. garlic salt
- 1 tsp. lemon juice
- Drizzle olive oil
- 2 Tbsp. tomato, diced
- 2 tsp. cilantro, chopped
- Salt and pepper, to taste
- 1/4 cup black beans, drained and rinsed
- 1/2 garlic clove, chopped
- Salt and pepper, to taste

Directions:

1. Preheat oven to 325 degrees F.
2. In a medium saucepan, heat olive oil over medium heat and add the garlic and half the onions and cook until translucent, about 2-5 minutes.
3. Add the black beans, turn heat the low. Stir occasionally and allow the beans to heat while you work on the filling.
4. Arrange corn tortillas in a single layer on a large baking sheet, and place in the preheated oven 2 to 5 minutes, until heated through.

5. In a medium bowl, mix avocado, remaining onion, tomatoes, garlic salt, pepper, lemon juice and a drizzle of olive oil.
6. Spread tortillas with avocado mixture, add black beans and top with cilantro.

Nutritional Information
- Calories: 377.1
- Total Fat: 18.3 g
- Saturated Fat: 3.4g
- Carbohydrates: 43.8 g
- Protein: 9.3 g

Vegan Style Shepherd's Pie

Ingredients:

Mashed potatoes:

- 5 russet potatoes, peeled and cut into 1-inch cubes
- 1/2 cup vegan mayonnaise
- 1/2 cup soy milk (or other milk substitute)
- 1/4 cup olive oil
- 3 Tbsp. vegan cream cheese
- 2 tsp. salt

Filling:

- 2 carrots, diced
- 2 stalks celery, diced
- 3/4 cup broccoli florets
- 1 tsp. Italian seasoning
- 1 clove garlic, minced
- 1/2 tsp. celery seed (optional)
- Pepper, to taste
- 1 (14 oz.) package vegan ground beef substitute
- 1 Tbsp. extra virgin olive oil
- 1 large yellow onion, diced
- 1/2 cup Cheddar-style soy cheese, shredded

Directions:

1. Place potatoes in a large pot, cover with cold water, and bring to a boil over medium-high heat. Turn the heat to medium-low and simmer the potatoes until tender, about 25 minutes. Drain and return to the pot.

2. In a bowl, combine the vegan mayonnaise, soy milk, olive oil, vegan cream cheese, and salt. Add to the potatoes mix with a potato masher until smooth and fluffy. Set aside.

3. Preheat the oven to 400 degrees F and grease a 2-quart baking dish.

4. In a medium skillet, heat the olive oil over medium heat. Add the onions, carrots, celery, and broccoli and cook for 10 minutes, or until softened. Stir in the Italian seasoning, celery seed, garlic, and pepper.

5. Reduce the heat to medium-low and crumble the vegan ground beef substitute into the skillet. Cook and stir, until the mixture is hot, about 5 minutes.

6. Spread the vegetable and "meat" filling into the bottom of the baking dish, and top with the mashed potatoes, smoothing them into an even layer. Top the whole pie with the shredded soy cheese.

7. Bake in a preheated oven until the cheese is melted and slightly browned, approximately 20 minutes. Remove and serve. Leftovers can be stored in an airtight container, in the fridge, for up to a week.

Nutritional Information (for 1/6th of the pie)
- Calories: 558.4
- Total Fat: 24.4 g
- Saturated Fat: 3.6 g
- Carbohydrates: 64.5 g
- Protein: 20.2 g

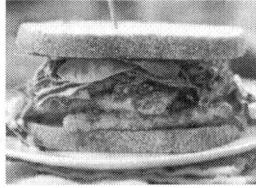

BBQ Tempeh Sandwiches:
Ingredients:
- 1/4 cup barbeque sauce, any kind
- 1/4 (8 oz.) package tempeh, crumbled
- 3/4 tsp. extra virgin olive oil
- 1/4 red bell pepper, seeded and diced
- 1/4 green bell pepper, seeded and diced
- 1/4 red onion, diced
- 1 Kaiser roll, split and toasted

Directions:
1. Pour the barbeque sauce into a medium bowl and crumble the tempeh into the sauce. Stir until the tempeh is covered, and let marinate for at least 10 minutes.
2. Heat olive oil in a skillet over medium heat. Add the onion, red, and green bell peppers. Cook for 4-5 minutes, stirring frequently.
3. Add the tempeh and barbeque sauce, stir and let cook until tempeh is heated through, about 8-10 minutes.
4. Spoon the bbq tempeh mixture into the toasted Kaiser roll and serve.

Nutritional Information
- Calories: 383.1
- Total Fat: 11.5g
- Saturated Fat: 2.1g
- Carbohydrates: 54.7g
- Protein: 15.2g

Easy Vegan Pasta with Pine Nuts

Ingredients:

- 1/2 cup farfalle pasta
- 1 roma tomato, diced
- 1 Tbsp. extra virgin olive oil
- 1 clove garlic, minced
- 2 Tbsp. fresh basil, cut into thin strips
- Salt and pepper, to taste
- 2 Tbsp. pine nuts

Directions:

1. Bring a small pot of salted water to a boil. Add pasta and cook for 8-10 minutes. Drain.
2. In a large bowl, gently toss the cooked pasta, tomatoes, olive oil, garlic and basil. 3. Season with salt and pepper and top with pine nuts.

Nutritional Information

- Calories: 275.6
- Total Fat: 14.8 g
- Carbohydrates: 32.2 g
- Protein: 3.4 g

HEALTHY EATING
on
a
BUDGET

Dexter Poin

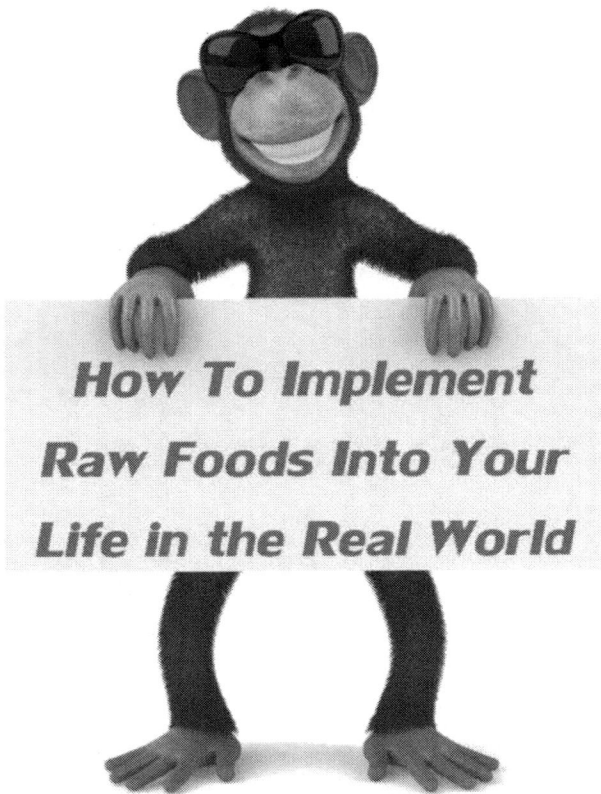

How To Implement Raw Foods Into Your Life in the Real World

DEXTER POIN

RAW FOOD

DEXTER POIN
RICE
50+ RICE COOKER RECIPES
RICE
100% VEGAN APPROVED!
BABY
QUICK AND EASY
COOKING FOR A HEALTHY
WAY OF LIFE!

Dexter Poin

VEGAN
SMOOTHIE
RECIPES #3

PLANT BASED
ANTI - INFLAMMATORY

50

Rice Cooker Recipes

RICE RICE BABY

Dexter Poin

The 2nd Coming
Of Riced

2

Made in the USA
Coppell, TX
23 August 2020